# 30 DAYS OF GLORY

## *A Life Changing Encounter*

Larry R. Taylor

Bloomington, IN  Milton Keynes, UK

*AuthorHouse™*  
*1663 Liberty Drive, Suite 200*  
*Bloomington, IN 47403*  
*www.authorhouse.com*  
*Phone: 1-800-839-8640*

*AuthorHouse™ UK Ltd.*  
*500 Avebury Boulevard*  
*Central Milton Keynes, MK9 2BE*  
*www.authorhouse.co.uk*  
*Phone: 08001974150*

*This book is a work of non-fiction. Unless otherwise noted, the author and the publisher make no explicit guarantees as to the accuracy of the information contained in this book and in some cases, names of people and places have been altered to protect their privacy.*

*© 2006 Larry R. Taylor. All rights reserved.*

*No part of this book may be reproduced, stored in a retrieval system, or transmitted by any means without the written permission of the author.*

*First published by AuthorHouse 8/15/2006*

*ISBN: 1-4259-5361-1 (sc)*

*Printed in the United States of America*  
*Bloomington, Indiana*  
*This book is printed on acid-free paper.*

*Library of Congress Control Number: 2006906839*

# Contents

Day 1:  Glory Encounters ................................................... 1
Day 2:  Anywhere But Here ................................................ 3
Day 3:  Lightning ................................................................ 6
Day 4:  Glory Folk .............................................................. 9
Day 5:  Show Me Your Glory ........................................... 11
Day 6:  The Goodness of God .......................................... 13
Day 7: Manifestations ....................................................... 15
Day 8:  Altered State......................................................... 17
Day 9:  Signs, Wonders and Miracles.............................. 20
Day 10:  Transformation .................................................. 23
Day 11:  Glory is the Goal................................................ 26
Day 12:  The Covenant of Goodness ............................... 28
Day 13: The Revival Connection..................................... 30
Day 14:  Testimonies........................................................ 32
Day 15: Gold .................................................................... 37
Day 16: Un-Filled............................................................. 40
Day 17: Is That You, Lord? ............................................. 42
Day 18: The Glory and the Gold...................................... 44
Day 19: The Latter House Glory ..................................... 46
Day 20: Meanwhile, Back at the Ranch........................... 50
Day 21: Revival!............................................................... 53
Day 22: Show and Tell ..................................................... 56
Day 23: Receive Ye the Holy Ghost................................ 59
Day 24: The Flood of Glory............................................. 62
Day 25: He Is Building A House ..................................... 64
Day 26: Tag, You're It!..................................................... 68
Day 27: He Is Not Finished.............................................. 70
Day 28: It's Going to Look Like Him.............................. 74
Day 29: "By My Spirit…"................................................. 76
Day 30: Arise Shine.......................................................... 79
Postscript........................................................................... 82

To my co-author, partner in ministry and life,
my wife Carol. Thank you.

## Introduction

For most of my life "glory" was one of those Church words that I heard used often but had no idea what it meant. This is, to some extent, a journal of what I have come to understand about His tangible here and now glory through my own personal encounters. A few years ago I asked the Lord to give me a definition of His glory that people could get hold of and really understand. I heard the Spirit of the Lord say, "the Glory is when God shows up and brings everything He's got with Him." My prayer is that as you read that you too will experience your own Glory Encounter.

*That the God of our Lord Jesus Christ, the Father of glory, may give unto you the spirit of wisdom and revelation in the knowledge of him:*
*The eyes of your understanding being enlightened; that ye may know what is the hope of his calling, and what the riches of the glory of his inheritance in the saints,*
*And what is the exceeding greatness of his power to us-ward who believe, according to the working of his mighty power,*
*That the God of our Lord Jesus Christ, the Father of glory, may give unto you the spirit of wisdom and revelation in the knowledge of him:*
*The eyes of your understanding being enlightened; that ye may know what is the hope of his calling, and what the riches of the glory of his inheritance in the saints,*
*And what is the exceeding greatness of his power to us-ward who believe, according to the working of his mighty power, Ephesians 1:17-19*

An amazing fact about God's revelation of His Glory is that two can be standing together and have a totally different read on what has happened. While others have seen more, some still only hypothetically theorize about the subject. The observations and accounts in this volume are what I have seen and heard.

*Father, glorify thy name. Then came there a voice from heaven, saying, I have both glorified it, and will glorify it again.*
*The people therefore, that stood by, and heard it, said that it thundered: others said, An angel spake to him.*
*Jesus answered and said, This voice came not because of me, but for your sakes.*
*Jonh 12:28-30*

The following messages are presented in a daily "devotional" format. I would suggest reading the message for the day and waiting in the presence of the Holy Spirit, perhaps with some worship music for background, allowing the revelation of His glory to come in His way and His time for you. The next 30 days could transform your life forever.

## Day 1: Glory Encounters

It was one of the most unusual weeks of my life. My wife Carol, our two daughters Leah and Anna, and myself were staying in what we affectionately called "the compound". It was actually a farm in East Texas that was the home of a group that had responded to the leading of the Holy Spirit in the 1970's to establish a community of believers. Many of the group lived on the farm in the middle of the pine forest in the middle of nowhere. The meetinghouse and guesthouse was at the center of the farm. We were there to conduct revival meetings for the group, but as the week progressed I realized that I was the one getting the download this time.

I had been prompted by the Holy Spirit to pray and ask the Lord to teach me more about His glory that week. Although I had been a pastor for over 13 years at that time and had a degree in religion from an accredited university, I had very little if any practical knowledge concerning the Glory of the Lord. To be honest, the concept was pretty much meaningless to me. If I thought about it at all, I just consigned it to an eventual state in heaven or defined it according to what I had heard my college professors say based on the Hebrew; "*kabod*- weightiness; heaviness; all that God is". That definition seemed to me to be fairly generic and irrelevant to everyday life.

I guess what I was expecting was a theological understanding so that I could preach intelligently on the subject. What I got was far different. By the end of the week at "the compound" I realized God had sent me to His school of reality. Rather than simply giving me high sounding words He gave me a week of hair-raising, nail biting, oh-my-gosh-what-was-that kind of experiences that I have since come to refer to as "glory encounters".

The lessons began with a focus on the Book of Ezekiel. God spoke to me to begin reading the whole book. As I began the project I first read the introduction in my study Bible, which said that among the Jews, Ezekiel is known as the prophet of God's glory. Ok, that answered the question, "why Ezekiel?" But much more was to come. In Ezekiel there are over 24 references to "glory". As I began to read the book I realized that much of it was beyond my comprehension. For a child of the 60's like me it sounded like the account of a really wild drug trip or multiple encounters with alien extraterrestrials.

Little did I realize that I was about to see some of the events from the Book of Ezekiel duplicated in the real world where I was firmly planted in religious ignorance. What began to unfold in my life that week was the realization that God's Glory is tangible and that every encounter with His Glory is a life-altering, revelatory, transformational event.

***You might want to start as I did reading the first chapter of Ezekiel in several translations.***

## Day 2: Anywhere But Here

The night was hot and still. The roar of multiple electric fans was only a polite gesture of resistance against the matching 95% humidity and 95 degree temperature of deep East Texas. Accompanying the packed crowd of sweaty worshipers was the wall-to-wall volume of the fan motor choir joined by fiddles, accordions, trumpets, saxophone, guitars, piano, drums, tambourines and the thump/thump rhythm of a Fender bass set on ten and a half. Seated on the front row next to me, Carol had one simple prayer, "Lord, get me out of here."

As soon as the silent words were prayer-breathed through her lips, it happened. The way she describes it, suddenly she was someplace else. I was standing next to her so we know her physical body didn't leave the place but she says it felt as if she literally left the room. I let her tell you the rest in her own words…

Carol; "I was hot and tired, but did not want to embarrass Larry by walking outside to cool off, so I closed my eyes and raised my hands to at least give the appearance of worship. All of a sudden I felt like I was being lifted up and the sound of the music around me faded. I had seen visions during worship before, but this was a new level for me. All I can say is that I felt like I was picked up and moved to a place very far away.

I was standing at the edge of a large ballroom, dressed in a beautiful, white ruffled ball gown. The ballroom had a high, vaulted ceiling and was so large that I could not see the other side. The room was brightly lit, but I could not see any chandeliers or other sources of the bright light that filled the room. I could hear waltz music, but could not see an orchestra.

As I stood there watching couples waltz to the beautiful music, I heard a voice say, 'Dance with me.' I turned around; there stood Jesus dressed in what I can only describe as a military officer's dress uniform. He took my hand and led me onto the dance floor. When we began to dance, I started laughing. I always loved watching people waltz, but never learned how myself.

As we danced, Jesus said, 'Isn't my bride beautiful.' I looked up and saw the back of an elegant, white wedding dress with a long, white lace train. Jesus was suddenly standing by the bride and turned her toward me. As I looked, I saw that the dress was empty. Jesus was smiling and said, 'Soon I will come to get my bride.'

Then I heard a loud, incredible sound. It sounded like singing with no discernable words. I know this sounds strange, but it was almost like I could taste the sweet sound. It got louder and louder until the sound shook my body and I fell to my knees."

As I fell to my knees in the vision, I felt myself physically falling downward. I could hear the thump, thump sound of the bass and just as quickly as I left, I was back in the meetinghouse in East Texas. I was so 'drunk' and had to sit down because every bone in my body felt like jelly. I could not talk very clearly for several hours and had the most peaceful sleep that evening. It has been several years since that experience, but I still hear the sound of heaven from time to time as I open my mouth to worship the Lord."

That same night several others had dramatic "Glory Encounters" as you will read in the following pages. This marked a major turning point for the two of us. For the first time in our lives The Glory of the Lord began to be an experiential reality rather than a theological concept.

## Day 3: Lightning

*"Going up and down among them were other forms that glowed like bright coals of fire or brilliant torches, and it was from these the lightning flashed. The living beings darted to and fro, swift as lightning." Ezekiel 1:13-14*

After the meeting a group walked over to the Pastor's home next door for coffee. One of the ladies in the parking lot came over to tell us that she had just seen a large bright angel following us as we walked. When we began to talk in the Pastor's living room there was a sense that something "special" was up.

One of the first to speak was the Pastor of The First Baptist Church in the nearby town. He began by saying that during the worship time he had one of the most unusual experiences he had ever had. He said he was caught up in the Spirit and taken into the heavenly realm. (sound familiar?) The first thing he noticed was that he heard very loud music, but it wasn't like earthly music. To his ears it sounded like every song and note that had ever been played or sung was being sounded at the same time. In spite of the multiple layers of sound, he reported that the music had harmony and rhythm but it's most obvious characteristic is that it was loud.

The Pastor went on to say that as he was caught up into this realm he not only heard this incredible sound but he also saw what appeared to be a ball of translucent light. Emanating from this ball of light were a vast array of colored points and flashes of lights. He described this glowing flashing orb in such vivid detail that we couldn't help but laugh because he was using such fluent and grand words we had to stop and ask him occasionally what the word he was using meant. Another man spoke up and said that he, too had experienced a similar vision during worship that evening.

The Pastor had barely completed his testimony of his remarkable experience when two of the teenage boys from the group burst through the door and into the heart of our conversation. They were pale, out of breath and both talking rapidly at once. As we slowed them down and were able to understand what they were saying, we were left speechless by what they had to say.

The boys told us that they were walking up the dirt road from the meetinghouse to their home when something darted out from behind the vehicle parked in front of the house. They both saw the same thing at the same time (not a vision). They described it as a figure that had the shape of a man but couldn't have been a man because it moved so fast. The figure was glowing with a bright light and in their own words they both said, "It looked like lightning flashing back and forth in front of us." The being darted several times in this manner and then darted down the road away from them and disappeared. Then the boys turned to me and said, "What was it? Was it an angel or a demon?" Being the all-knowing fully armed man of God for the hour I stared blankly back at them and responded, "I dunno!"

But I determined that before daylight I would have an answer and I would get back to them. I asked the Lord to give me insight into what was happening before the next nights meeting so that I could help these people (including myself) understand all that was happening among us and why. The first thing I did was to look up the word lightning in my Strong's Concordance. The first reference I turned to was, you guessed it, Ezekiel 1:13-14. This description fit perfectly what the boys had seen.

As I continued reading and meditating on what the Pastor reported I realized that what he had seen also matched in many ways the description of the things that the Prophet Ezekiel had described in Chapter 1:16-28. The culmination of this chapter is a record of Ezekiel's own "Glory Encounter". That's when it hit me—God was revealing His glory. As a group we were being led into our own Glory Encounter.

## Day 4: Glory Folk

As I continued to meditate the next day on what we were experiencing in "the compound", I noticed a magazine among some literature in the Pastor's office. It came from England and was the publication of a group there who called themselves "The Glory Folk". This group began in the 40's and continues to this day. Their distinctive has been the manifestations of the Holy Spirit that we have come to associate with revival. Their term for what we in the revival/renewal movement refer to as the manifestations is "the Glory". Their understanding is that when the manifestations begin, the Glory of the Lord is present.

The pieces of the puzzle were beginning to come together for me. God's glory really could be defined by "God showing up and bringing everything He has with Him". Visions, angelic encounters, laughter, falling under the weight of presence, miracles, signs and wonders are all manifestations of His Glory. When His Glory manifests anything can happen because we are talking about the actual presence of God being revealed in our midst.

Biblically I noticed a pattern to these Glory Encounters or maybe I should more correctly say a purpose. The Glory Encounters we were experiencing that week together in a group setting and the scriptural accounts of the great men and women of God who had these same type encounters shared some common characteristics.

Glory Encounters always involve a miraculous (supernatural) element. Signs, wonders, and miracles happen when God shows up. But these signs are not the Glory; they just alert us to the fact that the Glory of God is present. His Glory is God Himself. As God reveals Himself, He does what He is. His nature is revealed in His Glory, both His character and His power.

Perhaps most significantly for us, His Word is revealed. When He shows up He speaks. Out of Glory Encounters come revelation on which life times of ministry and purpose are built. As Ezekiel encountered the Glory of the Lord, God began to speak to Him concerning the fate of Israel and his call to the prophetic ministry. Ezekiel had a life altering experience. He was changed forever. The fate of a nation was wrapped up in that encounter. Nothing would ever be the same again. Glory Encounters are transformational. We are a people who are being transformed by real life encounters with His tangible Glory. Glory Folk.

***"But we all, with open face beholding as in a glass the glory of the Lord, are changed into the same image from glory to glory, even as by the Spirit of the Lord." 2Corinthians 3:18***

## Day 5: Show Me Your Glory

Moses had a personal encounter with God's glory. There was nothing theoretical or hypothetical about Moses' understanding of glory. He asked for it and He got it: a personal, tangible life-changing encounter with the manifested Glory of God.

*"And he said, My presence shall go with thee, and I will give thee rest.*
*And he said unto him, If thy presence go not with me, carry us not up hence.*
*For wherein shall it be known here that I and thy people have found grace in thy sight? is it not in that thou goest with us? so shall we be separated, I and thy people, from all the people that are upon the face of the earth.*
*And the LORD said unto Moses, I will do this thing also that thou hast spoken: for thou hast found grace in my sight, and I know thee by name.*
*And he said, I beseech thee, show me thy glory.*
*And he said, I will make all my goodness pass before thee, and I will proclaim the name of the LORD before thee; and will be gracious to whom I will be gracious, and will show mercy on whom I will show mercy.*
*And he said, Thou canst not see my face: for there shall no man see me, and live.*
*And the LORD said, Behold, there is a place by me, and thou shalt stand upon a rock:*
*And it shall come to pass, while my glory passeth by, that I will put thee in a cleft of the rock, and will cover thee with my hand while I pass by:*

*And I will take away mine hand, and thou shalt see my back parts: but my face shall not be seen." Exodus 33:14-23*

The revelatory encounter with His Glory began with a request. In the Kingdom of God, the principle is established for eternity; ask and you shall receive, seek and you shall find, knock and the door shall be opened to you. When you ask, be ready, because the encounter could be intense, personal and powerful perhaps even frightening to some degree. Few are prepared for the level of reality experienced when the Glory of the Lord manifests. When God gets real anything can happen and probably will.

Moses had a "Glory Encounter". Peter, James and John had "Glory Encounters" (Matthew 17). Paul had a "Glory Encounter" that changed everything. He was knocked to the ground and nothing was the same when he got up. His purpose, direction in life, even his name was changed. (Acts 9). Remember the principle of the Kingdom? Ask, seek, knock. "Show me your Glory, Lord."

## Day 6:  The Goodness of God

When Moses boldly asked to see the glory (Ex. 33), God's response was, "Ok, I will allow my goodness to pass before you." From this early encounter forward throughout scripture God's goodness and His Glory are seen as synonymous. The terms are used interchangeably at times. As I mentioned earlier in the introduction, I asked the Lord to give me a definition of His glory that people could get hold of and really understand. I heard the Spirit of the Lord say, "the Glory is <u>when God shows up and brings everything He's got with Him.</u>"

***"How God anointed Jesus of Nazareth with the Holy Ghost and with power: who went about doing good, and healing all that were oppressed of the devil; for God was with him." Acts 10:38***

Everywhere Jesus went He manifested the Glory of the Father. The tangible expression of that Glory is that good things happened. Everywhere Jesus went sick people were healed, demoniacs were delivered and provision was released. It's still the same. Everywhere Jesus shows up He manifests the Glory of the Father. Miracles, signs, wonders and supernatural events happen when the presence of God is manifested.

The manifested Glory of God is more than a mood or an atmosphere. His Glory involves the tangible revelation of His goodness. When God shows up He brings the atmosphere of heaven with Him. The earthly realm is invaded by the heavenly and God takes over. So another way of defining

His Glory is to say that it is when "God shows up and He takes over."

One of the most interesting miraculous events described in the ministry of Jesus is the transformation of water into wine at the wedding in Cana (John 2:1-11). The often-overlooked summary statement of that event says, ***"This beginning of miracles did Jesus in Cana of Galilee, and manifested forth his glory; and his disciples believed on him. (John 2:11)*** So, Jesus' miraculous act was specifically referred to as the manifestation of His glory.

When we use the term "doing good" in a modern religious context we are usually referring to a "good deed", some act of kindness done in the name of God, like feeding the hungry or clothing the poor or housing for the homeless. All these are important, effective and mandated by scripture. But they are not what Jesus did when the Bible says "He went about doing good". Every event or act of "goodness" on Jesus part was miraculous in nature. Check it out for yourself. Examine scripture and see if you can find one example of Jesus doing something "good" that wasn't miraculous in nature. When we ask, as Moses did, that God show us His Glory we should expect to see His goodness manifested in tangible, identifiable, miraculous events.

## Day 7: Manifestations

When God shows up and brings everything He's got with Him--anything can happen. The atmosphere of heaven invades the human realm, which can produce often unexpected and even startling results, especially for those unaccustomed to the degree of reality that God is willing to reveal. Sometimes I find it amusing to hear people praying fervently for God to show up and then be taken totally taken off guard, even offended by some of the things that happen when He actually does.

It seems that the human body goes into something of an overload mode when His Glory manifests. Strange things can happen. People often shake or fall simply overpowered by the experience. Tears are common, but so is laughter. The laughter is one of the more unexpected and puzzling results of His manifested glory for those who have a traditional rather than scriptural view of the atmosphere of heaven. Scripture says that in His presence is fullness of joy and at His right hand are pleasures for evermore.

***"Thou wilt show me the path of life: in thy presence is fullness of joy; at thy right hand there are pleasures forevermore." Psalm 16:11***

Joy has a sound. It's called laughter. When God shows up, one of the things He brings with Him is joy and real joy produces laughter. This brings up an important point. In the denominational church I was brought up in, emotions and emotionalism were seen as highly undesirable (but only in a religious setting). Meetings in which tears or laughter or any strong emotion were evident were discouraged if not out rightly forbidden. These outbursts were derisively referred to as "emotionalism".

After years of observing a varied number of responses to the presence of God I have come to the conclusion that what is happening is not emotionalism in the purest sense. What is happening is a "spiritual" experience that has a profound effect on the emotions (as well as the physical body for that matter). When the Holy Spirit moves on an individual, every component of our being is affected; mind, body, and soul. The encounter has a profound effect on the emotions, but it is not emotional in origin. The distinction is important if you feel that emotions are entirely subjective and not "real" from a scientific, materialistic view. However, something very "real" is happening in a realm that touches the human heart like nothing else can and that has a remarkable outcome in the emotions.

After all, we are talking about an encounter where we are exposed to a level of the reality of the living God that few ever experience. People often faint, scream, shake or cry in the presence of rock stars or great leaders. How much more should that be expected in the presence of Almighty God the creator of the universe. When God gets real, so do we.

***"Whom having not seen, ye love; in whom, though now ye see him not, yet believing, ye rejoice with joy unspeakable and full of glory" 1Peter 1:8***

## Day 8: Altered State

*"For it is the God who commanded light to shine out of darkness, who has shone in our hearts to give the light of the knowledge of the glory of god in the face of Jesus Christ." 2 Corinthians 4:6*

The highest manifestation of the Glory of God is seen in the face of Jesus Christ. According to 2 Corinthians 3:18 "But we all with unveiled face, beholding as in a mirror the glory of the Lord, are being transformed into the same image from glory to glory, just as by the Spirit of the Lord." The Holy Spirit reveals the face of Jesus Christ. The outcome is that we are transformed into the image we behold—we shine!

In attempting to describe what a person experiences in a Glory Encounter, the best description seems to be that we are in an altered state. What is experienced is real, but in another realm from normal sensory perception. Jesus becomes so real that His tangible presence becomes the focus of all senses. We feel His touch, hear His voice, see His face, and smell His aroma and it is just as real and identifiable as sitting next to a life long friend and engaging them in normal conversation. But it is on another level. We are usually not seeing with our natural eyes or hearing with our ears. Yet we are hearing and seeing.

Recently I was listening to the radio when the host of the program signed off by saying "I will see you tomorrow". Now everyone listening knew we wouldn't "see" him with our eyes and yet that is the only way to communicate the thought being expressed. "See you tomorrow" on the radio means we will hear his voice and experience his on air presentation audibly. In a similar manner, when we "see His glory" or "hear His voice" or "feel His presence" it is a real tangible experience that can only be conveyed in words that approximate the encounter. The encounter is so unique it defies description—but one thing is certain—When we see Jesus we are transformed by the experience and we are never the same again!

God is looking for those that are willing to embrace the full expression of His Glory. A heart that is open to receive is the prerequisite. A few months ago the Holy Spirit defined the manifested Glory of the Lord for me in the following terms: "When God shows up and brings everything He's got with Him!" Unfortunately, many choose to narrowly specify to God what they are willing to receive. The degree to which we are able to embrace the full expression of His glory will determine the extent to which we benefit from the encounter. His desire is to transform us from "glory to glory". He wants to take us to places we never dreamed we could go. But if we limit His access to our lives or limit our receptivity to the expressions of His glory that He chooses to use then we cut ourselves off from the changes that He desires to bring.

When God shows up in His glory He is in control and we have lost control. He takes over. Our minds are affected— our thoughts, perceptions and senses are overloaded. Our physical bodies are often impacted by the tangible manifestation of His Glory; some shake, some fall, some laugh, some cry. Many experience a trance-like or dream-like state. Some hear and/or see angels. Sometimes physical stuff happens. I have seen oil form on people's hands or "glory dust" appear and cover whole rooms and everything in them. Clouds, lights and sweet aromas have all been reported by those are caught up in His glory. Scripture says that the ultimate manifestation of the Glory of the Lord is seen in the face of Jesus Christ.

*"For God, who commanded the light to shine out of darkness, hath shined in our hearts, to give the light of the knowledge of the glory of God in the face of Jesus Christ." 2Corinthians 4:6*

When we see Jesus we have seen the ultimate expression of the Glory of the Father revealed by the Holy Spirit. All the fullness of the Godhead dwelt bodily in Him. It is the assigned task of the Holy Spirit to reveal Jesus to us, thus revealing the Father. When we see Jesus, we have seen the Father. We often opt for complexity when trying to express and experience all that God is, when what we really want is reality. The reality of Jesus. God with us. Somehow we mistakenly believe that in order for something to be significant and important it must also be complex. The truth is, the closer we get to Jesus the clearer things become. Our minds become untangled, our thoughts become more cogent. Issues are suddenly resolved in a flash of divine revelation. Direction comes and decisions are easy. Even more astounding...circumstances change, physical healing takes place and provision miraculously materializes. Freedom and emotional healing come. The manifested presence of Jesus brings joy and peace like no other experience can and it changes us in ways that defy description.

## Day 9:  Signs, Wonders and Miracles

*"Ye men of Israel, hear these words; Jesus of Nazareth, a man approved of God among you by miracles and wonders and signs, which God did by him in the midst of you, as ye yourselves also know"  Acts 2:22*

*"How God anointed Jesus of Nazareth with the Holy Ghost and with power: who went about doing good, and healing all that were oppressed of the devil; for God was with him." Acts 10:38*

*"This beginning of miracles did Jesus in Cana of Galilee, and manifested forth his glory; and his disciples believed on him."  John 2:11*

There are several key terms used in the verses above that are intertwined and have a direct impact on experiencing and understanding the Glory of the Lord. In Jesus dwelt the fullness of the Godhead bodily.  When we see Jesus we are seeing the Glory of the Father revealed.

In that revelation comes the demonstration of the goodness of the Father.  Everywhere Jesus shows up good things happen.  As Moses asked to see the Glory, God said I will show you my goodness. So Jesus reveals the true nature and character of the Father by revealing His goodness.

In Jesus' ministry, this goodness takes the form of the miraculous.  Miracles are the acts of goodness that Jesus did which scripture says, "manifested forth His Glory". If you examine what Jesus actually did as described in the Gospel you will fail to find one single act of "goodness" that did not involve the miraculous.

Signs and wonders are God's way of getting our attention and saying, "Hey, something is going on here, you need to pay attention ." The signs and wonders themselves are not the focal point, instead they are used to draw our focus to what God is saying and doing.

The burning bush with Moses and the star that guided the Magi to baby Jesus are both examples of signs and wonders that served to get somebody's attention so that they could hear what God was saying or take notice of what He was doing. The bush caused Moses to turn aside and hear the voice of God. The star led the Magi to Jesus. Once the star got them to Jesus, it's purpose had been served. The significant event was Jesus; the star was simply God's way of getting them to where they needed to be. On the day that Solomon's Temple was dedicated the day was marked by the visitation of God's glory. The visitation also included the appearance of smoke that filled the building as well as the priest being overcome by His presence and rendered unable to stand.

I have seen God use a number of signs, wonders and miracles to draw attention to what He is saying and doing in my life. I have seen manifestations of oil, feathers and unusual displays of light. I have lost count of the number of healing miracles as well as miracles of provision that I have witnessed. I believe that we will see even more displays of God's unlimited creative ability as we draw closer to the end of the age. God is good.

There are many signs and wonder associated with the manifestation of the Glory, but the focus is on seeing and hearing the voice of God through the presence of Jesus

Christ. Miracles happen because that is what Jesus does when He gets real. The tangible manifested Glory of the Lord is all about Jesus getting real and revealing who He really is. God is good.

## Day 10: Transformation

*"Now the Lord is that Spirit: and where the Spirit of the Lord is, there is liberty.*
*But we all, with open face beholding as in a glass the glory of the Lord, are changed into the same image from glory to glory, even as by the Spirit of the Lord."*
*2 Corinthians 3:17-18*

Changed-metamorphoō (gk)
**Thayer Definition:**
1) To change into another form, to transform, to transfigure
   1a) Christ appearance was changed and was resplendent with divine brightness on the mount of transfiguration

There is a dynamic involved in an encounter with the Glory of God that always produces change. Most often the change is radical. A persecutor of the faith goes in zealously pursuing Christians for the express purpose of killing them in order to wipe out what he considers to be a rapidly spreading heresy. He comes out with a changed named, a follower of Jesus Christ and an apostle of the group he was trying to wipe out. Radical change.

It is important to understand the dynamic of how this radical change occurs so that we too can experience the transformation of ever increasing glory. First, we are told in 2 Corinthians 3:17 that the Lord is the Spirit. The work of the Holy Spirit is never to be relegated to some less than essential element of the Christian experience. The Holy Spirit is the Spirit of the Living God. The Holy Spirit is

God's presence in man. We are told in Colossians 1:27 that "Christ in us is the hope of glory". The anointed one, Christ, and His anointing in us is our hope of the revelation of the true Glory of the Lord. Without the work of the Holy Spirit we cannot experience the Glory of the Lord.

There is no competition in heaven. The Father, Son and Holy Spirit are in perfect harmony and unity. One heart, one mind, one purpose; the Godhead moves, acts and speaks as one. Jesus said if you have seen me you have seen the Father. He goes on to say that He is sending "another". His work is clearly outlined in John 16. In this widely misinterpreted and misapplied passage Jesus makes it clear that the Holy Spirit has come to reveal the glory by passing on what the Son has received from the Father.

***"Howbeit when he, the Spirit of truth, is come, he will guide you into all truth: for he shall not speak of himself; but whatsoever he shall hear, that shall he speak: and he will show you things to come.***
***He shall glorify me: for he shall receive of mine, and shall show it unto you.***
***All things that the Father hath are mine: therefore said I, that he shall take of mine, and shall show it unto you."***
***John 16:13-15***

As we continue in 2 Corinthians we see that we are "beholding" the Glory of the Lord "as in a glass" or "through a mirror". In other words, we see the Glory but it's not like we see normally. We are seeing through Jesus as revealed by the Holy Spirit.

*30 Days of Glory*

As we see Jesus for who He really is, the result is change. We are transformed into the image we see. It is not just a one time experience or encounter. It is described as being "from glory to glory". This is a continuing transformational process that produces in us the character, nature and mind of Christ.

When we see Jesus the savior, we are saved. When we see Jesus the healer, we are healed. When we see Jesus the provider, provision manifests. Even more incredibly, we see that the Holy Spirit working in and through us can lead others to this same saving and healing knowledge.

As if to make sure there is no mistake about it, the passage in 2 Corinthians ends with these words, "by the Spirit of the Lord." The revelatory work that produces this transformation is the work of the Holy Spirit.

## Day 11: Glory is the Goal

*"For all have sinned, and come short of the glory of God"*
*Romans 3:23*

This verse is seen as the definitive description of the biblical view of sin. The word sin (*hamartano-gk*) literally means to miss or fall short of the mark. Then to underscore the meaning *"hustereo"* is used which also means, "to fall short". The word picture is of an archer who is aiming for a bulls-eye but the arrow falls short of the intended target.

The part of this scripture that caught my attention recently is not the falling short portion, but the goal itself. Like many others my attention has been on the definition of sin. I think that speaks volumes. The Churches' focus has been on sin, whether abstinence from sin or participation in sin, the focus has still been the same: **sin**. If we follow the principle that we become like what we focus on the most, then it is inevitable that as we remain preoccupied with the topic it will dominate our behavior.

What caught my attention recently is the goal. The goal that is held up as the standard is "the glory of God". Sin is falling short of "the glory". His glory is the goal, not just the minimum conduct required to be acceptable.

For some time now I have been defining "glory" as when God shows up and brings everything He's got with Him! The manifested Glory of the Lord is His presence, His Kingdom and His demonstrations revealed. His glory is His nature, character and power on display.

When we see that Glory is the goal, our view of sin is radically altered. What we are shooting for in our personal lives as well as our corporate gatherings is the reality of His manifested glory shining through these earthen vessels.

We are not merely seeking the highest expressions of behavior modification and human will power; our goal is to reveal the true presence, nature, character and power of God. That's not hard, THAT'S IMPOSSIBLE!! Only by His glory working in us can we express His glory. We have to receive it in order to display it.

It is time to raise the bar. Sin is not just what we don't do, the behavior we avoid. Sin is the failure to actively display all that God is. We may not hit the mark every time, but if we are not even shooting for that mark we will surely never hit it. If we focus on the true goal, His glory, just by focusing on the target we break the cycle of preoccupation with sin. We also get the focus off of our own inadequacy and begin to seek His fullness. Even if we don't hit the mark every time, at least we will some of the time.

It is important to state the obvious. Without the Holy Spirit working in us to impart His glory, we can never achieve the goal set before us. That is the reason Paul said, ***"This I say then, Walk in the Spirit, and ye shall not fulfill the lust of the flesh." Gal. 5:16***

## Day 12: The Covenant of Goodness

*"I will gather them out of all countries, whither I have driven them in mine anger, and in my fury, and in great wrath; and I will bring them again unto this place, and I will cause them to dwell safely:*
*And they shall be my people, and I will be their God:*
*And I will give them one heart, and one way, that they may fear me forever, for the good of them, and of their children after them:*
*And I will make an everlasting covenant with them, that I will not turn away from them, to do them good; but I will put my fear in their hearts, that they shall not depart from me.*
*Yea, I will rejoice over them to do them good, and I will plant them in this land assuredly with my whole heart and with my whole soul.*
*For thus saith the LORD; Like as I have brought all this great evil upon this people, so will I bring upon them all the good that I have promised them." Jeremiah 32:37-42*

God's intention is to have a people set aside for one express purpose and that is to reveal His Glory in the earth. In order for that to have full expression, there must be a people who are recipients of his goodness. In Jeremiah 32, God speaks of the day and the people coming that will be marked by an everlasting covenant that is established to do them good. This people will have a heart knowledge rather than a head knowledge. They will also be marked by a reverential awe of God that produces obedience from the heart. But what will be most striking about this covenant is that God will be actively, even aggressively "doing them good".

Acts 10:38 tells the story of how "God anointed Jesus...who went about doing good and healing all those oppressed of the devil". The New Covenant precisely fits the prophetic description of Jeremiah of this coming covenant of goodness.

*"For the earth shall be filled with the knowledge of the glory of the LORD, as the waters cover the sea." Habakkuk 2:14*

The knowledge of the tangible, observable, manifested Glory of the Lord will fill the earth. That Glory will be demonstrated and put on display through a covenant people who are a demonstration of the goodness of God "in the land of the living". David cried out for the goodness of God in the land of the living. That is the promise of God to us and the innate yearning in every believers heart imparted by the Holy Spirit.

*" I had fainted, unless I had believed to see the goodness of the LORD in the land of the living." Psalm 27:13*

"The land of the living"--you know; where you live, at your house, in your body, in your family, in your bank account, at your job--the reality of Jesus manifested in the real world. That is our inheritance and our hearts cry! His Glory manifest in our lives and the result is changes in everyday practical situations. The goodness on display reveals the true nature of the living and loving God who desires a people to bless. He rejoices to do us good. It is not a bother or an imposition, it is His revealed will and intention to be a good Father to His sons and daughters.

## Day 13: The Revival Connection

***"To the intent that now unto the principalities and powers in heavenly places might be known by the church the manifold wisdom of God." Ephesians 3:10***

The Church of Jesus Christ fully functioning, fully empowered, filled with His Glory on display for all to see; that is Gods intention for His people. The modern expression of the Church in most western nations falls so short of that goal that it would appear to be impossible to achieve. As we say in Texas, "you can't get there from here."

With men it is impossible, but with God all things are possible. A group of 500 people witnessed Jesus ascension back to the throne. He told them to go to Jerusalem and wait for the coming of the Holy Spirit. Of that group, 120 showed up for the meeting. They were obediently gathered in the upper room on the Jewish feast day of Pentecost when the promise came. A Glory Encounter miraculously transformed one hundred and twenty people that day. A rag tag group of religious, political and social misfits scarred and scared by the rejection of friends and family and the execution of their leader suddenly became a group of bold witnesses who turned the world upside down with their message and it's wonder working power.

The most startling change was in their leader, Peter. He had denied Jesus and gone back to fishing. Apparently he comprehended very little of what He had witnessed in the previous three years as he and the twelve had followed Jesus day after day. He still was confused and filled with shame at his own personal failure and the incongruities of Jesus' earthly ministry. Suddenly, this fear filled failure rose and boldly addressed over 5000 people to clearly and unequivocally declare that what they were seeing was the fulfillment of the words of the prophet Joel and the promise of Jesus that the Holy Spirit would be poured out on mankind. It's almost as if you could her Peter exclaim; "OH! NOW I GET IT! This IS that spoken by the prophet…"

The change was not just a revelatory internal change. Not only did the knowledge come but also so did the power. The words that the 120 now spoke not only testified to the transformational work in their own hearts, they also now carried the same authority and power that Jesus had displayed to heal the sick and deliver those in bondage. The Church was born in a Glory Encounter that revealed Jesus through a group of people by the work of the Holy Spirit. It is my belief that revival is the restorative work of the Holy Spirit to bring a carnal and fallen Church back to that same transformational encounter to produce the same results today.

## Day 14: Testimonies

Authors note:
This marks the mid-way point through the 30 Days of Glory. Beginning in the next message (Day 15) and following are a personal account of a deeper understanding of the Church and the Latter House Glory. God is taking His people somewhere and He wants you fully aware of the destiny and purpose that is your inheritance as His children. I hope you will join me for the next 15 days that could change your life. In preparation you might like to beginning reading the books of Haggai, Ezra and Nehemiah.

***"But we all, with open face beholding as in a glass the glory of the Lord, are changed into the same image from glory to glory, even as by the Spirit of the Lord." 2Corinthians 3:18***

*TESTIMONIES:*
The topic of God's glory is so awesome.

I've had visions over the years of the glory of Jesus- the first led me to getting saved just on 30 years ago this month... my that time has flown by.

One time in church I had three little snippets of heaven. In one of them everyone was going to a big stadium. I asked people what was happening and someone said, "We're going to see Father". The way he said "Father" was full of awe, respect, honour, warmth, love...

So many people take coming into God's presence so lightly, almost like being in a football match.

Yes there is joy. But there is a world of difference between the joy of the Lord and just silliness.

We also need to bring honour and love to the Father.

We've experienced joy in our church lately. Not laughter as such but the happiness of being God's people in god's presence. It's truly wonderful...

Many treat the manifestations as some kind of entertainment, or as a validation of their church/ ministry. If we get the gold dust we must be good.

For over 12 months our church had a confetti manifestation. Often in a morning, I would come into the building and there would be confetti scattered around one part of the building.

Whether people didn't believe me or they thought confetti was less impressive than gold I don't know, but we didn't get the streams of people coming in to see the manifestation.

But this was God getting my attention in an extended period of discouragement, reminding me that He is in control and He is leading us on.

The manifestations are there to point us to God, not to point to themselves.

K.B.

"Hi Larry,

Well, now let's see. I am not sure if you are still looking for Glory encounters, but just in case, for your book report... I think I have been walking in one since I heard you preach. I am not sure where even to begin. Kim and I led 7 people to the Lord that week that I was on Cape [Cod] and hearing you--coupla alcoholics, an oxicoton addict, a coke addict, and 3 children. ... And when I returned to NYC on Thursday for a dog-sitting job...the Lord spoke into my heart about a retreat. ...OMG. All so timely... It all worked out and I feel God's hand and Face so much, I feel like I might pop. It's all wonderful...the kingdom is JOY... Thank you." S.

"I wish that I could remember the first time I met you... it has been a day or two ago! I do remember meeting in the small pastor's office at New Life for prayer before the service. By the time I had come to the service, revival had begun. There were already many manifestations that God had poured out, however there were many more to come. The glory of God is like that for me. Just about the time I think I have seen, felt, or understood as much as I can about the glory of His grace, He reveals another wonderful part of Himself.

The gold was such a small part of the manifestation of God's glory. There were healings and restorations in many lives. And once God began to truly show himself, the battle was then intensified. Some paid a great price for their efforts, though none as great as our Savior! While the final outcome of that battle has not yet been seen, the victory is already secure. It only remains for us to be a part of it. One of the theme songs that emerged from those days in Weatherford, Texas was "Jump." Tragically, too few people are willing to do that!"

Blessings to you,

D.E.



Hey there Larry!

Please: keep 'em comin'!!! I'm sending them out to people I know just as fast as I get them from you. All that I can say is "Thanks".

I believe as we are reading these day by day, our expectation is being stretched, enlarged, expanded, and lifted, raised and kicked up to a higher level than we had ever imagined possible.

Preparing us Spirit, Soul and Body.

Thanks again,

K.



I would like all to know what God has done for me. During a service at Toronto Airport Christian Center, we were being ministered to by Daniel Garza. God truly[sic] uses him to heal the broken and physical healings. Daniel had given me a scripture that touched my heart. I went over to him to Thank him for the scripture. In the process of giving Daniel a little of my life and what I needed from the Lord to further His work for the broken in my area. Daniel ministered to me that I needed healing in my ears before I can adminster [sic]healing to others. He anointed[sic] my palms and my ears. He then blew into my ears and they popped open. I now can hear to a much bigger capacity than I have ever been able to. I can hear back round noises and things are clear as a bell!!!!! I have been hearing impaired since birth. At the age of 4 years old I was involved in a car accident in which a tire caught hold of my ear instead of my head and ripped my ear half way off. It became harder for me to hear out of the left ear. I had to go to many hearing doctors as a child. I had to wear a hearing aid in school and all the children use to make fun of me and call me names. I threw the hearing aide out. I couldn't bear the anquish[sic]. I learned to read lips and strain to listen to hear people. It never stopped the ability for me to play music and sing. I was always on key. There has been some healing to my ears over the years. Nothing major just bits and pieces were restored. Now, I have been restored and the Lord has released me to pray for healing to others. I am Blessed and Loved by My Father. All I want is to show His Glory and Love to others and be transparent to minister the work of the Lord for the coming harvest. The fields are white!!!!!! D.G.

## Day 15: Gold

*"But as it is written, Eye hath not seen, nor ear heard, neither have entered into the heart of man, the things which God hath prepared for them that love him.*
*But God hath revealed them unto us by his Spirit: for the Spirit searcheth all things, yea, the deep things of God."*
*1Corinthians 2:9-10*

Have you ever experienced an extended dry season? For me, it was about 1998. Nothing seemed to be happening. The tremendous rush of progress and blessing that flowed into my life following a revival encounter in 1993 seemed to have run its course. I thought maybe revival was over for me. It sure seemed that way.

I prayed. I put it honestly to God. If what I had already seen and heard in the early days of the '90s was all that was available, then I would be happy and content for the rest of my life with what I had already experienced. Most people live their whole lives and at best see one or two mighty moves of God. Many leaders from the past have gone happily to their reward having only witnessed one true revival in their lifetime and books and stories are still being written about their lives. I would certainly praise Him for the multiple outpourings I have witnessed during my lifetime.

But something wouldn't let me adopt that posture. I just felt there should be more. What the prophets had spoken concerning the great revival to come certainly seemed to point to more than what I had already witnessed. Somehow the Spirit of God within me was drawing me on in spite of my dryness of soul.

Then I began to hear reports, mainly from a friend of mine from South Africa, that something new was beginning to happen in the meetings he was conducting. The joy of the Lord that was such a hallmark of the move we had experienced in '93 was still in evidence, but there was a new wave of signs being released as well. To be specific, gold was "happening".

My friend, John Sheasby, reported to me that gold colored dust was appearing on people in his meetings. In some cases people's dental work was turning gold. Increased healing miracles and miracles of provision were also breaking out. I was greatly encouraged by his reports and others I began to hear about a fresh release of the anointing.

I started to seek the Lord and ask Him for this same release in my life. I have discovered a principle of the Kingdom. God doesn't show partiality. If one of His children has received something from Him, then it is available to all of His children. Rather than be jealous about what He is doing in someone else's ministry and grumble and murmur about my own condition, I rejoice because I know that if He is doing something for them then the same thing is available for me. I ask for it.

The answer didn't come instantly, but when it came boy did it really shake things up in my life! In the months following my initial seeking of God in this matter I really began to understand the concept of "eye hath not seen". The fresh release of anointing and the new levels of glory

*30 Days of Glory*

that began to flow into my life were things I couldn't have asked for because I didn't even know they were available. Most significantly, I discovered that not only was God not through yet, He had only just begun and the best was yet to come!

## Day 16: Un-Filled

The testimonies that I was hearing about gold dust (glory dust) and gold teeth accompanied by dramatic healings and provision were a great encouragement to me after the extended period of drought I had been in. I remember several times when I was preaching during the high point of revival for me, from '93 to '97, that I would often say I'd rather be driving a truck than go back to dead religion. Well, sure enough, God gave me that opportunity. In 1998 I got so dry I started driving a truck and waiting to see what happened next. As I heard these new reports towards the end of that year I began to seek the face of God again about revival.

Some friends in ministry were gathering at my home on Sunday afternoons in those days. We all began to pray and ask God for a fresh anointing and these new manifestations. One of my good prophetic friends had a word about the gold at one of those home meetings and an admonition to pray one more time. We did, and we went one more step; we actually began to look in each other's mouths to see if there were any "dental miracles". Sure enough, my friend's wife had what looked like a filling that was gold in color and in the shape of a cross. Several others that day reported fillings that changed colors or glory dust on their skin or clothing. My wife, Carol, said her mouth had "that dentist office taste".

One of the ladies with small children had to leave early before we prayed. I knew she would be interested so I called her on the phone the next day about what had happened and suggested she might check her own teeth. She said she would and hung up the phone. In just a matter of seconds the phone rang and it was her. I could tell she was very excited. She breathlessly explained to me that just a couple of weeks prior to the Sunday meeting she had taken her oldest son to the dentist for four fillings. After she hung up the phone, she had checked his mouth first. He didn't have any gold fillings—HE DIDN'T HAVE ANY FILLINGS AT ALL! The fillings that the dentist had done just a few weeks before were gone, and where they had been, were perfectly whole teeth.

Now this really got my attention. I was beginning to get breathlessly excited myself. I started sharing with everyone I knew what we had seen. That's when things started to multiply. It seemed that every time we started talking about these unusual signs and wonders they manifested. On the phone, in conversations, in meetings, whatever the setting—the gold manifested.

## Day 17: Is That You, Lord?

*"The silver is mine, and the gold is mine, saith the LORD of hosts." Haggai 2:8*

Because I first heard of the gold manifestations from a good friend of mine, I wasn't as skeptical of the reliability of the reports as I normally would have been. I was even more encouraged when I heard that the gold teeth had also been reported in some meetings at the Toronto Airport Christian Fellowship. As with all new things I hear about, I had two basic questions: Is it you Lord? & What are you saying?

Again the Lord led me to my old reliable friend, The Strong's Exhaustive Concordance. I looked up references to gold and for some reason I was particularly drawn to Haggai 2:8 where the scripture says, "the silver is mine, and the gold is mine, saith the Lord of Hosts". That settled that issue for me. If the Bible says it is His then that is all I needed to know.

The second question, however, is where it got really interesting for me. When God uses dramatic signs and wonders it is to get our attention. He usually wants to get our attention so that we will focus on what He is saying or doing. For instance, the burning bush is a good example. Because Moses turned aside and looked at the bush that was burning but not consumed, God spoke to Him. The revelation that came from that encounter provided Moses with a map for the rest of His life and the destiny of the Jewish people. Another good example is the Star of Bethlehem. The star was not the focus. The star led the Magi to Jesus. Jesus was the focus; the star was simply God's sign to get them where they needed to be to worship the newborn King of Kings. Dramatic signs, wonders and miracles are to get our attention so that we will focus on what God is saying and doing.

***"Ye men of Israel, hear these words; Jesus of Nazareth, a man approved [attested, NKJV] of God among you by miracles and wonders and signs, which God did by him in the midst of you, as ye yourselves also know" Acts 2:22***

I wanted to know the significance of the gold manifestations prophetically. Too often people treat very significant events that are happening in the Body of Christ as if they were just a passing fad for their entertainment. When this happens the full impact of what God wants to accomplish is lost. Instead of seeking God in the manifestation, immature believers often focus on the manifestation and fail to recognize the real importance of what they are experiencing. Like Peter on the Mount of Transfiguration (Matt.17: 3-5), they want to build a monument to the occasion as a memorial to their participation rather than understand the true meaning of the moment. It is interesting to note that on that occasion God himself spoke unequivocally and said; "this is my Son in whom I am well pleased, listen to Him!" The message was: FOCUS ON JESUS—LISTEN TO HIM!!

## Day 18: The Glory and the Gold

The prophet Haggai was sent by God to stir the people to return to work on the rebuilding of the Temple. During the restoration period after Israel's return from the Babylonian captivity, the people had grown weary and discouraged. In their malaise they turned aside from their destiny and purpose and began to focus on their own houses. This led to the condition described in the first chapter of Haggai where the people were living in paneled houses while the Temple was in a state of total neglect. Haggai's call and admonition was for the people to return to their destiny and true calling. God was not finished with His house!

As I began to meditate on Haggai I realized that in the context of the answer to my first question (was the gold manifestation of God?) came the answer to my second question as well (what are you saying, Lord?). It hit me like a brick. The condition of Israel at that time paralleled my own condition and many that I knew in the Body of Christ. Revival had come. We had gotten off to a great start. However, opposition came. The work was difficult and often our motives were questioned. The continual backpressure and the vehement opposition from those in the Church had greatly hindered the work of revival. Because of my own feelings of personal rejection, I had shut down. Like Peter who returned to fishing, I drove a truck. The effect in my life was perfectly described by the prophet.

***"Thus speaketh the LORD of hosts, saying, This people say, The time is not come, the time that the LORD's house should be built.***

*Then came the word of the LORD by Haggai the prophet, saying,*
*Is it time for you, O ye, to dwell in your ceiled houses, and this house lie waste?*
*Now therefore thus saith the LORD of hosts; Consider your ways.*
*Ye have sown much, and bring in little; ye eat, but ye have not enough; ye drink, but ye are not filled with drink; ye clothe you, but there is none warm; and he that earneth wages earneth wages to put it into a bag with holes.*
*Thus saith the LORD of hosts; Consider your ways.*
*Go up to the mountain, and bring wood, and build the house; and I will take pleasure in it, and I will be glorified, saith the LORD.*
*Ye looked for much, and, lo, it came to little; and when ye brought it home, I did blow upon it. Why? saith the LORD of hosts. Because of mine house that is waste, and ye run every man unto his own house." Haggai 1:2-9*

I heard clearly the implication of my dry condition. I had given up and quit. As a result, I was suffering. It was time to return. God started something and He wasn't finished yet. Revival was not then nor is it now over. God is building His house and His city and He has called us to that destiny. Church, it is time to return to your calling and destiny.

## Day 19: The Latter House Glory

In the message of the prophet Haggai, there is a clear declaration of God's plan for Israel emerging from slavery in Babylon to their destiny in the land. The first priority was establishing a city, Jerusalem, and then rebuilding the Temple. The message to the people was that the project they were involved in needed completion. His promise to them was that the provisions necessary were available and that He was capable of equipping them for the task. They were working in the shadow of the former Temple built by Solomon. It's chief characteristic was that it was practically gold and silver-plated. Haggai assures the people that God has got the gold. The job can be done, now is the time and they are the people.

*"For thus saith the LORD of hosts; Yet once, it is a little while, and I will shake the heavens, and the earth, and the sea, and the dry land;*
*And I will shake all nations, and the desire of all nations shall come: and I will fill this house with glory, saith the LORD of hosts.*
*The silver is mine, and the gold is mine, saith the LORD of hosts.*
*The glory of this latter house shall be greater than of the former, saith the LORD of hosts: and in this place will I give peace, saith the LORD of hosts." Haggai 2:6-9*

In reading Haggai 2:6, I realized that the prophet had hit the fast forward button. He was no longer talking to a people long ago. He was talking to a generation who would see their whole world shaken. He was talking to a generation who would see an unprecedented worldwide revival break out. He was talking to us.

*"See that ye refuse not him that speaketh. For if they escaped not who refused him that spake on earth, much more shall not we escape, if we turn away from him that speaketh from heaven:*
*Whose voice then shook the earth: but now he hath promised, saying, Yet once more I shake not the earth only, but also heaven.*
*And this word, Yet once more, signifieth the removing of those things that are shaken, as of things that are made, that those things which cannot be shaken may remain.*
*Wherefore we receiving a kingdom which cannot be moved, let us have grace, whereby we may serve God acceptably with reverence and godly fear:*
*For our God is a consuming fire." Hebrews 12:25-29*

"The glory of the latter house"—Those words jumped off the page. We are being built into a house: His House and a Temple–His temple. Not only are we being built into a dwelling place for His Glory, but that Glory (the latter house glory) is going to exceed anything and everything He has ever done up to that point. What an incredible time we live in.

*"we are laborers together with God: ye are God's husbandry, ye are God's building.*
*According to the grace of God which is given unto me, as a wise masterbuilder, I have laid the foundation, and another buildeth thereon. But let every man take heed how he buildeth thereupon.*

*For other foundation can no man lay than that is laid, which is Jesus Christ.*

*Now if any man build upon this foundation gold, silver, precious stones, wood, hay, stubble;*

*Every man's work shall be made manifest: for the day shall declare it, because it shall be revealed by fire; and the fire shall try every man's work of what sort it is.*

*If any man's work abide which he hath built thereupon, he shall receive a reward.*

*If any man's work shall be burned, he shall suffer loss: but he himself shall be saved; yet so as by fire.*

*Know ye not that ye are the temple of God, and that the Spirit of God dwelleth in you?*

*If any man defile the temple of God, him shall God destroy; for the temple of God is holy, which temple ye are." 1Corinthians 3:9-17*

*"And are built upon the foundation of the apostles and prophets, Jesus Christ himself being the chief corner stone;*

*In whom all the building fitly framed together groweth unto a holy temple in the Lord:*

*In whom ye also are builded together for a habitation of God through the Spirit."*
*Ephesians 2:20-22*

*"Ye also, as lively stones, are built up a spiritual house, an holy priesthood, to offer up spiritual sacrifices, acceptable to God by Jesus Christ.*

*Wherefore also it is contained in the scripture, Behold, I lay in Zion a chief corner stone, elect, precious: and he that believeth on him shall not be confounded.*

*Unto you therefore which believe he is precious: but unto them which be disobedient, the stone which the builders disallowed, the same is made the head of the corner,*

*And a stone of stumbling, and a rock of offense, even to them which stumble at the word, being disobedient: whereunto also they were appointed.*

*But ye are a chosen generation, a royal priesthood, a holy nation, a peculiar people; that ye should show forth the praises of him who hath called you out of darkness into his marvelous light:*

*Which in time past were not a people, but are now the people of God: which had not obtained mercy, but now have obtained mercy." 1Peter 2:5-10*

## Day 20: Meanwhile, Back at the Ranch

*"And they overcame him by the blood of the Lamb, and by the word of their testimony; and they loved not their lives unto the death." Revelation 12:11*

The understanding of the prophetic significance of the gold manifestation found in Haggai emboldened me as I continued to share with others what we were seeing. The more we talked about the gold, the more it happened. I noticed something else happening almost immediately. Everywhere the gold manifested it increased faith to receive miracles of healing and provision.

What began with that small group in my living room on a Sunday afternoon began to quickly spread as I determined to share with everyone I knew what was happening. That decision led me back into the calling of God on my life to revival ministry. It also led me back to "deepest darkest" East Texas where God had begun to teach me about His Glory several years before. I picked up where I left off.

For years a group of pastors had been meeting weekly in the small lumber town of Kirbyville, Texas. Long before it was fashionable, their simple goal was to pray for revival in their community. They were a diverse group; Baptist, Methodist, Pentecostal and Independent Charismatic meeting each week for breakfast and then prayer. I had gotten to know most of them several years earlier during a round of revival meetings at "the compound".

*30 Days of Glory*

I followed the leading of the Spirit to drive down from Fort Worth just for their meeting and to share what had happened in my living room a few weeks earlier. As we gathered in his office, the pastor of First Baptist Church turned to the other men and said that I had something to share and then he turned the meeting over to me. I told them about the gold manifestations, the young man who had received the dental miracle, and the connection I saw with the prophecies of Haggai.

As I finished speaking I was wondering what their reaction was going to be. These men had a wonderful fellowship but they were from a wide spectrum theologically. The pastor of First Baptist broke the silence. He said simply, "well, would you pray for us?" Would I? You bet I would! I led them to pray a simple prayer that I have since led thousands to pray with me: "Lord, we are Your Temple; Lord, I am Your Temple; Fill Your Temple with Your Glory—now."

I handed one of the pastors a flashlight and encouraged him to check out the teeth of those gathered. A nervous laughter spread through the group. I could tell this was a bit of a stretch for some of these men of God. But sure enough, the first man checked had gold fillings. The pastor with the flashlight exclaimed to the others; "They are turning gold right now." All the inhibitions and religious protocol went out the window. Like a group of curious little boys, we crowded around this one poor guy's opened mouth to watch in amazement as his dental work turned gold right in front of our eyes.

Several of the men reported changes in their dental work that day. It was a Wednesday so most of them had mid-week services that night. As they shared in their Churches reports began immediately of more gold teeth. The move was on!

## Day 21: Revival!

*"But Peter, standing up with the eleven, lifted up his voice, and said unto them, Ye men of Judea, and all ye that dwell at Jerusalem, be this known unto you, and hearken to my words:*
*For these are not drunken, as ye suppose, seeing it is but the third hour of the day.*
*But this is that which was spoken by the prophet Joel;*
*And it shall come to pass in the last days, saith God, I will pour out of my Spirit upon all flesh: and your sons and your daughters shall prophesy, and your young men shall see visions, and your old men shall dream dreams:*
*And on my servants and on my handmaidens I will pour out in those days of my Spirit; and they shall prophesy:*
*And I will show wonders in heaven above, and signs in the earth beneath; blood, and fire, and vapor of smoke:*
*The sun shall be turned into darkness, and the moon into blood, before that great and notable day of the Lord come:*
*And it shall come to pass, that whosoever shall call on the name of the Lord shall be saved." Act 2:14-21*

As the reports of gold teeth and glory dust began to spread through the piney woods of deep East Texas, so did revival fire. The first Wednesday night after the pastor's meeting in Kirbyville several of the fellowships involved reported outbreaks of dental miracles, healing and other unusual signs.

The men of God leading the Churches were not unprepared for revival. Several had been experiencing a move of God for a number of years. They were eager and hungry for this fresh outbreak. Two groups in particular, The New Covenant Fellowship of Jasper and Bonami Missionary Baptist Church of Kirbyville, were already conducting joint Sunday night services. I was invited to share at one of these services.

It was a small building, that would hold 100 if completely full, and it was packed with over 100 people. Most of those present had already heard about the gold and had come to see what God would do next. He didn't disappoint us. God showed up in His glory. His tangible presence was as thick as the 100% humidity in the air. The air-conditioning and the sound system were overloaded as God's people joined in worship with a country flavor.

When I say God showed up in His Glory, this is what I mean. His multi-dimensional nature was on full display. Several reported being saved, others returned to the Lord in this atmosphere of love and forgiveness. Many were instantly healed of serious illnesses and conditions. There were numerous reports of unusual signs and wonders. Some who had been adamantly opposed to the manifestations of the Holy Spirit were powerfully filled and began to have manifestations of their own. The unity of the Spirit in the bond of love was the order of the day. As men of God opened their arms to receive each other and what was happening in their midst, congregational distinctions melted with the summer heat, and we merged into one people, the people of God.

It was evident to all that we were in the midst of a fresh outpouring of the Holy Spirit in revival. The meetings were extended to the weeknights and continued for several weeks. In the next section I will detail more of the remarkable miracles we witnessed in Jesus name. But first let me point out the direct connection between signs, wonders, miracles and revival. What began with the gold teeth, the Holy Spirit multiplied into a full blown revival in just a matter of days. The message that came forth was right out of Haggai. God was building His Temple (us) and filling it with His Glory (Him), and we were experiencing the results—His goodness on display (salvation, restoration, unity, miracles, signs and wonders) in the "land of the living" real world.

## Day 22: Show and Tell

*"And I, brethren, when I came to you, came not with excellency of speech or of wisdom, declaring unto you the testimony of God.*
*For I determined not to know any thing among you, save Jesus Christ, and him crucified.*
*And I was with you in weakness, and in fear, and in much trembling.*
*And my speech and my preaching was not with enticing words of man's wisdom, but in demonstration of the Spirit and of power:*
*That your faith should not stand in the wisdom of men, but in the power of God."*
*1Corinthians 2:1-5*

This revival was happening in the most unlikely place among the least likely people. We were in a rural setting in an area of Texas that most people don't even know exists. The Church that was hosting the meetings was a part of a Baptist denomination that didn't fellowship with other Baptist, much less Pentecostals, Charismatics, or Methodist. But here we were night after night coming together in unity in His presence to experience the manifestations of His Glory.

One of the remarkable things I observed from the beginning of the gold manifestations was how quickly the sign spread when people talked about it. The more they talked the more it happened. And I am not talking about some contrived manipulative verbal ambush, just regular everyday conversations would lead to reports of gold fillings or glory dust showing up. Distance seemed to be no barrier either as there were several reports of people talking on the phone and someone on the other end seeing an immediate manifestation.

In this atmosphere of miracles, many came for healing. Jesus, The Healer, manifested in a remarkable way. One of the first was a man healed of lung cancer who had already had one lung removed. The doctors said he had only days left. His health was restored and he lived several more years after these meetings. The Pastor of the host church was healed of palsy that he had carried since childhood. A man confined to a wheel chair for over a year, paralyzed with no feeling or movement below the waist, received both feeling and movement in one of the meetings.

One night during a time of powerful release, a lady got up out of her seat and made her way to the aisle. I motioned for her to come forward. She obediently came to the front. As I laid my had on her forehead, she fell to the floor immediately and began to speak in tongues. Her Baptist pastor came over to me and jokingly said that he would have gladly paid me $100 for that one. When I asked why, he said that this woman had been very vocal in her criticism of what was happening and didn't want any part of it. The next night when she came in the building her whole countenance had changed. She was laughing and singing and praising God. Later in the service, I asked her to come and share with the congregation what had happened. As she testified the truth came out. I had totally misread the situation. She wasn't getting up to come and receive prayer. She was trying to make her way to the bathroom. She just didn't want to embarrass herself so when I called her forward she came. But the Holy Spirit did His work anyway. She was full of thanksgiving for the immediate joy and peace that flooded her as she received the fullness of the Baptism of the Spirit. In a Glory Encounter sometimes even your enemies become your friends.

# Day 23: Receive Ye the Holy Ghost

*"But as many as received him, to them gave he power to become the sons of God, even to them that believe on his name:*
*Which were born, not of blood, nor of the will of the flesh, nor of the will of man, but of God." John 1:12&13*
*"He said unto them, Have ye received the Holy Ghost since ye believed? And they said unto him, We have not so much as heard whether there be any Holy Ghost." Acts 19:2*

I am frequently asked, "What is the key to revival?" It would be impossible to nail it down to one thing. Unfortunately, many have tried to produce a plan or procedure to follow to insure instant revival. They never work. Revival is a sovereign work of God in the hearts of man. However, there is one common denominator I have observed anywhere true revival breaks out and His Glory is manifested.

During the '90's I had the opportunity, as many others did, to go to the places where powerful moves of God had broken out. I was in several Rodney Howard-Browne meetings in a number of locations. I visited Toronto twice for a week each time and Brownsville Assembly of God in Pensacola, Florida for a week. This was in addition to the meetings that I was holding during the same period where many of the same things were occurring.

I asked the Lord what these diverse ministries had in common that released the Glory in revival. The answer came very simply; <u>they all said yes</u>. When God showed up and the Spirit began to move the leaders and the people involved had the same response. In spite of their theological, sociological and stylistic differences they all said yes. And not a grudging, I guess it will be ok, kind of yes; but an emphatic aggressive enthusiastic YES!!

The Holy Spirit will show up wherever He is invited (sometime even where He is not invited), but He will remain where He is celebrated rather than merely tolerated. Being in the traveling ministry I am often the guest in homes and churches. Some people go out of their way to show true hospitality and gladly receive you. On those occasions I feel welcome and want to stay. Others are barely able to conceal their feelings of imposition through thinly veiled politeness. I am sure you have had the same experience as you have been a guest in someone's home. It doesn't take long to know if you are really welcome or just being tolerated.

Many have had a one time or brief exposure to revival. The Father in His mercy and sovereignty will pour out His Spirit in revival glory anywhere people are gathered in His name. Where He makes His habitation instead of just a visitation is where people make room for Him and allow Him to have His way.

Ultimately, one of the central issues faced in revival is control. When God shows up for real, He expects to be treated like God. He is funny about that. When God shows up in His manifested tangible Glory, He takes over. It is no longer our plans and preferences that matter, but we are being led, directed and empowered by the very presence of the living God.

Have you received the Holy Spirit since you believed? Don't be too quick to answer. I mean have you fully embraced Him as the presence of the living God and accepted the complete array of all that He is capable and eager to do? Having had a taste of what that reality is like, are you eager for more? Have you settled in your heart the issue of whether or not you really want Him or are you still a bit embarrassed about what happens when He really gets hold of people and has His way? Have you really received Him?

## Day 24: The Flood of Glory

*"For the earth shall be filled with the knowledge of the glory of the LORD, as the waters cover the sea." Habakkuk 2:14*

God's plan is to have a people in which His Glory resides as a permanent habitation. This people will be blessed with supernatural tangible evidence of the presence of God. His nature and character will be their nature and character. His miracle working power will be on display through signs wonders and miracles done at the hands of His servants. His goodness will be their never-ending inheritance.

This people will be a direct fulfillment of the promise made to Abraham that in his seed all the peoples of the earth would be blessed. His Spirit will flow through this people and be a river of healing to the nations to fulfill the words of the prophet Elijah.

This people will be the Body of Christ fully functioning, fully equipped and Holy unto Him. This people will be transformed by the work of the Holy Spirit into the image of Jesus Christ. This people who were not a people will be made into a Temple not made with human hands but who are the workmanship of God almighty. They will be a dwelling place of His Glory for all the nations of the earth to behold.

The Glory of this Latter House will cause the nations of the earth to come to the desire of all nations. As the heavens and earth shake and kingdoms and nations fall, that which cannot be shaken shall remain. In the midst of great darkness a great light will once again shine. And the nations of the earth will be drawn to it's shining. A city set on a hill that cannot be hidden. A people filled with the Glory of the Lord, King Jesus.

Can this be? Is it possible? Will the glory of this latter house really exceed the glory of the former?

*"Then he answered and spoke unto me, saying, This is the word of the LORD unto Zerubbabel, saying, Not by might, nor by power, but by my spirit, saith the LORD of hosts."*
*Zechariah 4:6*

## Day 25: He Is Building A House

Authors note: In these last 6 installments are the summary conclusions that have been grafted into my heart during the past 13 years of encountering His Glory. Hopefully they will be helpful to you in seeing God's destiny for you personally and His Church in the significant days ahead.

*"For thus saith the LORD of hosts; Yet once, it is a little while, and I will shake the heavens, and the earth, and the sea, and the dry land;*
*And I will shake all nations, and the desire of all nations shall come: and I will fill this house with glory, saith the LORD of hosts.*
*The silver is mine, and the gold is mine, saith the LORD of hosts.*
*The glory of this latter house shall be greater than of the former, saith the LORD of hosts: and in this place will I give peace, saith the LORD of hosts." Haggai 2:6-9*

As in the days of Nehemiah, Ezra, Haggai and Zechariah God is involved in a massive building project. He is building a city and a temple. Jerusalem was to be rebuilt as a prosperous city of peace. It was to be a place where the nations could interact with and observe God's blessing on His chosen people. Jerusalem was to be a place of commerce, society and protection from enemies.

In the midst of the people, at the heart of all they did, was to be a structure, the Temple, which was at the same time the symbol and the reality of God's abiding presence. In the same way Moses spoke with God about leading the Israelites into the land of promise, the first issue that was dealt with was God's abiding presence. Both Moses and God agreed that there was nothing to distinguish Israel from all the other nations on the earth unless the presence of the Lord was with them. Moses went so far as to say that he was not going unless God was going with them. What is the distinguishing characteristic of His Church that is to separate us from all the other institutions, religions, ethnic groups, social organizations and humanistic philosophies? Immanuel, God is with us.

In most modern day moves of God there seem to be two distinct phases. First, there is the initial outpouring. During this phase there is a spontaneity and dependency on the presence of God. Usually this is a time of unknown men being used in powerful ways that challenge the old established order of things. The focus is on personal experience, rather than institutions and organizations. As things progress, there is usually a gradual shifting into the second phase that includes more focus on organization, plans, buildings and financial stability. Unfortunately, this shift is often accompanied by the loss of vision and purpose that birthed the move in the beginning stages.

Surprisingly, I don't find scriptural reason to resist the shift itself. However, I do believe the transition is often made from operating in the Spirit in the first phase to carrying out the vision in the flesh in the second phase. The result is simply that old cold dead institutions built on the traditions of men are replaced by new cold dead institutions built on updated technologically enhanced versions of the same old tired traditions of men.

There is, with out question, the necessity for human accessibility to the presence of God. He wants His glory to be observable and the benefits clearly verifiable. This requires human contact and visible displays of blessings. Provision, abundance, health and other signs of well-being and security are not in opposition to the purposes and plans of God, rather they are a validation and confirmation of His goodness. However, when man takes over in manipulative, greedy, materialistic pride, God's glory is replaced by the glory of human achievement. Inevitably, what results in the latter case is so far inferior to what God had planned that it can only be described as sinful.

First, a place must be established for His permanent abiding presence so that the personal reality of His Glory is continually manifested in open displays of His goodness. Then, an equally significant place is to be established in which human interaction and social activity take place with the abiding presence of God as the context for community life. Having begun in the Spirit will we be perfected in the flesh? No, but too often that is the methodology applied by the Church. Both the Temple and the City are to be built according to the purpose, plans and power of the Builder and filled with His abiding presence.

Let me make this a little less esoteric and more down to earth. When Carol and I were dating in the early 1970's, we were invited to hear a speaker who was going to be at a place called the "Shepherd's Inn" in east Texas. We were involved in the local version of the Jesus Movement in those days and were always looking for a place where God would "show up".

We weren't disappointed that night. Although we had never heard of him, had no idea who he was, (he was a lot older than most of the crowd), we were blessed by the power and reality of the teaching and the depth of understanding of the Word of God this man displayed. There were maybe 30 or 40 present at the most, but in those days we considered that a pretty good size meeting. The speaker's name? Kenneth Hagin.

As most of you who are reading this know, Pop Hagin established a school, publishing, radio and TV ministries that grew enormously and remain today as a legacy to the faith movement that he pioneered. In the early days of his long ministry, the life, revelation, and glory were present, just as in the latter years. The ministries that Brother Hagin established and built later became the occasion for millions of people world-wide to be exposed to what began simply as revelation in his heart.

***"For he looked for a city which hath foundations, whose builder and maker is God."***
***Heb 11:10***

## Day 26: Tag, You're It!

*"Know ye not that ye are the temple of God, and that the Spirit of God dwelleth in you?" 1Corinthians 3:16*
*"What? know ye not that your body is the temple of the Holy Ghost which is in you, which ye have of God, and ye are not your own?"*
*1Corinthians 6:19*
*"And what agreement hath the temple of God with idols? for ye are the temple of the living God; as God hath said, I will dwell in them, and walk in them; and I will be their God, and they shall be my people."*
*2Corinthians 6:16*
*"Now therefore ye are no more strangers and foreigners, but fellow citizens with the saints, and of the household of God"*
*Ephesians 2:19*
*"Ye also, as lively stones, are built up a spiritual house, an holy priesthood, to offer up spiritual sacrifices, acceptable to God by Jesus Christ."*
*1Peter 2:5*

One of the tendencies I've noted among many Christians is to believe that for something to be significant or important it has to happen to somebody else somewhere else at some other time. Great encounters with God; miracles, signs, and wonders always seem to happen to some one special in some unusual locale. After all, if it were really important how could it be happening to me? "If God wanted to do something significant this would be the last place he'd choose." Seems so humble, doesn't it? But it is false humility. In 2 Corinthians 4:7 Paul specifically says that God has chosen to reveal His

Glory in earthen vessels so that it is obvious that the power is from Him and not us. The real question is: "If not now, when? If not here, where? If not you, who?"

When it comes to great faith, one of the most difficult and often hidden issues of the heart has nothing to do with our belief in God's ability. His sufficiency is a given accepted without question. The real issue is often; "but can God do it through me?" Believing that God can use you, that is where real faith comes in. We are the people, the city and the house. In the New Testament there is no doubt concerning the true nature of the coming Temple. We are it. You are it!

If the knowledge of the Glory of the Lord, the tangible manifested Glory of God, is going to fill the earth then guess where He will show up in your town. That's right, it'll have to be you. If you are a believer then you are the vessel that God has chosen to pour His Glory into. Let me ask you a question. Is where you live on a map? Is it in the earth? Then guess what, His Glory is going to be revealed through His Temple where you live and that means you are the one responsible for revealing His Glory where you live.

King David cried out to God to see the Glory of the Lord in the 'land of the living'. The land of the living: at your house, on your job, in your family, in your bank account, at your address. "Father, we are your Temple. Fill Your Temple with your Glory. Lord, I am your Temple. Fill your Temple with your Glory, NOW!"

## Day 27: He Is Not Finished

*"Thus saith the LORD of hosts; Consider your ways.*
*Go up to the mountain, and bring wood, and build the*
*house; and I will take pleasure in it, and I will be glorified,*
*saith the LORD." Haggai 1:7-8*

After the meetings in East Texas in spring of 1999 the renewed work spread to other locations in Texas: Weatherford, Granbury, Clyde, and Sweetwater. What I saw happening led me to the conclusion that the prophetic mission and message of Haggai was equally important today in the Body of Christ as it was then in the people of Israel. I saw that the gifts and callings of God poured out in the atmosphere of revival and Glory Encounters are without repentance. The anointing doesn't go away, we do. More than once I heard Pastor John Arnott of the Airport Christian Fellowship in Toronto say that if you believe revival is over, then unfortunately for you it is.

As I ministered in one out break after another beginning in 1999 through the summer of 2000, I soon realized that I had totally misread the heart of God. Revival wasn't over. The lifestyle of walking in the Spirit of God is to be a progressive "glory to glory" experience. He has called us to an end-time work, and He is not finished with that work. Though many who initially experienced the outpouring of the Holy Spirit in revival have moved on to other things, God has not completed the purpose for which He poured out His River; the healing of the nations.

*30 Days of Glory*

In Weatherford we had a series of spontaneous unplanned meetings that extended for four months. Night after night the Glory manifested. Dramatic healings were reported from conditions such as sleep apnea, post-polio syndrome, cancer and hepatitis-C. Hundreds of people reported normal amalgam fillings in their teeth turning gold. Many told of visions, dreams and dramatic revelatory encounters. The local and national news media caught wind of the event and published numerous newspaper articles from San Diego to Houston to Boston. We were featured on live call in secular radio broadcast in several major markets. The CBS-TV affiliate in Dallas did a feature story on the revival including a live satellite feed from the parking lot on the night the broadcast aired. All this happened with no advertising, just spreading the story by word of mouth. Most importantly for me, night after night lost men and women, young and old found Jesus. Those who had fallen away from their first love were restored in an atmosphere of forgiveness and joy.

The experience of one youth group sums it up for me. They had come from the nearby city of Granbury to Weatherford to be in the meetings. The group witnessed the "glory dust" and had some powerful personal encounters with the Holy Spirit. They returned from the meetings and were back in their regular High School environment the next day. The Pastor's wife from their church just happened to be substitute teaching in one of the classes that day. At the end of the day's lesson she allowed them to talk quietly among themselves. Several of the teenagers from the group started excitedly telling others what had happened in the meetings. Because of the educational guidelines, the teacher couldn't join in the conversations, but she listed with interest as they talked about seeing the gold dust and being overcome by the power of the Holy Spirit. Sure enough, the gold began to manifest right there in the High School classroom.

One young man was listening intently. He was not in the Church group. As a matter of fact he was a hard core "Goth" dressed in black from head to toe. He approached the teacher and began to talk. Surprisingly he told her that he believed that this really was God. However, he added he knew that God would never do something like that (the gold dust manifestation) for "someone like me." Since the young man initiated the conversation the Pastor's wife now felt free to talk with him. She pointedly said, "I believe he would." The young man protested and again expressed his doubt that God would do something for someone who had messed up as badly as he had. Finally the teacher couldn't contain herself any longer. She called his name and said, "I know He would because you are covered in gold right now." The young man looked at his clothing for the first time and realized that he too was covered in what looked like multicolored glitter from head to toe.

The story doesn't stop there. By God's providence the meetings closed out in Weatherford and another series of meetings quickly began in Granbury in the same church that this youth group was from. The "Goth" came to the meetings with the youth group and was saved. He brought his family. Brothers and sisters were saved. Finally his mother and father came and were saved too. And as if to top it all off with a heavenly exclamation mark the father was healed of cancer.

Wherever I travel I find people who have been touched by the power of God and then gone on to experience rejection, disappointment or failure. Like the Israelites of Haggai's generation, they discovered the purposes and plans that God has for His people has enemies. Unfortunately, those enemies can be as readily found on the inside of the Church as on the outside "in the world'. Wounds are inevitable. Hurts come. The resulting feelings and experiences have left thousands immobilized and neutralized in a state of introspection, or worse; despair and depression. Some are overtaken by overt sin, others simply by ambivalence.

God's word to you is "I'M NOT FINISHED WITH YOU YET!" Right now He is calling you back to your destiny in His plan. One final point from the experience of the Israelites on this subject really excites me. He doesn't wait until the house is finished to bless those who return to the work. In Haggai 2:16-19 it is clear that from the moment you return to His calling and destiny on your life, the blessings of His presence begins to flow.

*"Consider now from this day and upward, from the four and twentieth day of the ninth month, even from the day that the foundation of the LORD's temple was laid, consider it.*
*Is the seed yet in the barn? yea, as yet the vine, and the fig tree, and the pomegranate, and the olive tree, hath not brought forth: from this day will I bless you." Hag 2:18-19*

## Day 28: It's Going to Look Like Him

*"Now if any man build upon this foundation gold, silver, precious stones, wood, hay, stubble;*
*Every man's work shall be made manifest: for the day shall declare it, because it shall be revealed by fire; and the fire shall try every man's work of what sort it is.*
*If any man's work abide which he hath built thereupon, he shall receive a reward.*
*If any man's work shall be burned, he shall suffer loss: but he himself shall be saved; yet so as by fire.*
*Know ye not that ye are the temple of God, and that the Spirit of God dwelleth in you?*
*If any man defile the temple of God, him shall God destroy; for the temple of God is holy, which temple ye are." 1Corinthians 3:12-17*

God is building His house. There is no other foundation that can be laid than that which is laid, which is Jesus Christ. After the foundation of the revelation of Jesus is laid, then we have a choice. What are we going to use to construct this building?

Wood, hay and stubble are still used as ingredients for building material in certain regions of the world. We have a name for the buildings constructed in this manner. They are called mud huts. Straw is mixed with mud and walls go up. Maybe it covers the need for basic shelter, but it's certainly not a temple. It may be what everyone else is building, but it is still a mud hut. It may be an elaborate design, but it's still a mud hut. It may be the biggest in the village, but it's still a mud hut. Gold, sliver, precious stones speak of a Temple. A Temple fit to contain the Glory of The King. We choose.

A few years ago I met a very interesting man who worked with marble. His specialty was counter tops and bathtubs. He took me to his warehouse where he kept the marble stored until time to craft it into whatever he was making. He was especially proud of several large wooden shipping crates that contained very special marble from Israel known as Jerusalem marble. He explained to me that this was especially valuable because of it rarity but also because of the way it was extracted.

One of the most desirable characteristics in marble is that consistent patterns and colors run through the stone so that when it is assembled in the final use it matches from one piece to the next. In order for this consistency to be present the stone slabs have to be cut in the quarry from the same vein of marble preferably at the same time and then packed and numbered together so that the slabs are as close to a perfect match as possible.

As I was listening to this skilled artisan describe this process I realized something about the Temple that God is building in us. Jesus is the cornerstone, the first piece that sets the pattern and standard for the rest of the structure. The Father wants the building to match. He wants it to look like Jesus throughout. From start to finish, He desires that the materials match. Anywhere you look in the building, you should see Jesus.

*"A Song of degrees for Solomon. Except the LORD build the house, they labor in vain that build it..." Psalm 127:1*

# Day 29: "By My Spirit…"

*"Now the Lord is that Spirit: and where the Spirit of the Lord is, there is liberty.*
*But we all, with open face beholding as in a glass the glory of the Lord, are changed into the same image from glory to glory, even as by the Spirit of the Lord."*
*2Co 3:17-18*

Comparing the current condition of the Church in much of the western world to the prophecy of the Latter House Glory in Haggai, an honest assessment would have to say "you can't get there from here". But that fails to take into account what God says through the prophet Zechariah.

*"Then he answered and spoke unto me, saying, This is the word of the LORD unto Zerubbabel, saying, Not by might, nor by power, but by my spirit, saith the LORD of hosts."*
*Zechariah 4:6*

The glory of the Lord poured out in His people will be a work of the Holy Spirit, not of men. Only a transformational work of the presence of God can bring about the degree of change required for the Church, The Temple of God, to reflect and reveal His true nature, character and power. Through the revelatory work of the Holy Spirit we will be transformed into the image we are beholding, the glory of the Lord in the face of Jesus Christ. This move of God on His people will not be the result of methodology, technique, style, technology, or education. It will not be earned, deserved, or achieved—it will be received.

A very good friend of mine, Steve, loves to say, "It's the anointing that makes the difference." Several years ago he went to Mexico on a ministry trip. The Pastor that took Steve on the trip also was acting as his interpreter. They reached a city on the western coast of Mexico where they were scheduled to minister in a small church for just one service. The guide/interpreter had double booked for the Sunday, so that he was speaking in another church at the same time. He left Steve to speak in this city alone with no interpreter (unknown to Steve) and no one in the congregation that spoke English. Steve's Spanish skills were limited to a few phrases he had learned by listening to preaching and interpreters in his own meetings. He knew "fuego"(fire), "venga Espiritu Santo" (come Holy Spirit) and "Gloria" (glory) and that was about it.

He felt impressed of the Lord just to get up and say the words he knew. So he just began repeating the phrases he knew in Spanish. In just a few minutes the Holy Spirit fell on the people and the fire of God broke out—shouting, laughing, people falling under the power of God and the glory dust was everywhere. When the meeting was over Steve and the other Pastor left almost immediately for their next engagement.

Three or four years went by and Steve never heard anymore from that fellowship. I invited Steve to go with me on a trip to Mexico with another friend, Daniel. Daniel had made arrangements for us to be in this same city. As we were driving to the church Steve told us the story and wondered out loud if it might be the same church he had been in on that first trip. Sure enough, as we pulled up to the Pastor's home Steve recognized it as the same place.

When we were greeted at the front door by the Pastor's wife she excitedly exclaimed "Esteban! (Steve!)" She began to rapidly tell us of a dream she had three nights earlier where she saw Steve coming with us back to their church. She had not known he was on the trip with our group. Finally she got to the most amazing part of the story for me. She said that their church had never been the same since that Sunday when Steve first ministered. The visitation of the Holy Spirit that day was so strong that it sparked a revival that completely transformed their small struggling group into a vibrant growing fellowship. Language barriers, human limitations, no matter what barriers exist—God is able!

## Day 30: Arise Shine

*"Arise, shine; for thy light is come, and the glory of the LORD is risen upon thee."*
*Isaiah 60:1*

As we behold Jesus, we are transformed into His likeness by the work of the Holy Spirit. Because it is the glory of the Lord that is revealed in the face of Jesus Christ we are transformed into a vessel of His glory. We shine with the imparted Glory of the Lord It is not possible to remain passive after encountering the manifested Glory of God. An extreme reality requires an extreme reaction.

Several years ago, I was ministering in an Assembly of God Church in San Diego, CA. It was on a Sunday night and I was preaching on the subject of the Glory of the Lord. As I was preaching I began to get an impression from the Lord of a very large bonfire built around the city. I am from Texas and what I saw was something along the lines of the huge structurally engineered bonfire built every year by the students of Texas A&M prior to the annual football rivalry with University of Texas. It is an assembly of telephone pole size logs constructed specifically for the purpose of making an impressive fire. In the vision I saw this fire igniting into a ring of glory that engulfed the city of San Diego.

As I was preaching this message, there was a group of about 14 youth seated close to the front of the auditorium. To me they seemed to be very restless. They were on the edge of their seats nervously shifting around occasionally whispering to one another. Being the "discerning great

*30 Days of Glory*

and mighty man of God for the hour" I once again totally misjudged the situation. I thought they were anxious for me to get through so that they could get outside and do the important teenager stuff, like talk and their cell phones "like, 'ya know". Boy, was I wrong.

What I didn't know was that these kids had just returned from a trip to Pensacola, FL where they had attended revival services at Brownsville Assembly of God. As I was talking about the Glory, they knew exactly what I was talking about and were just in a hurry for me to get the preaching out of the way so they could get in the zone. I finally finished and gave the altar call for those who wanted to receive the Glory. All fourteen of the group jumped from their seats and ran to the front.

As they ran to the altar I realized my mistake and in a flash of true discernment heard the heart of God. The Spirit spoke to me, "I want to meet them with the same intensity they have come to meet me." A Holy Ghost bomb exploded in my chest. I jumped from the platform and shouted at the top of my lungs "FIRE!" As soon as the sounds left my lips the group instantly and violently were thrown to the floor by the power of God. All went down immediately without me ever touching them. For the remainder of the night into the early hours of the next morning those kids remained on the floor under the power of the Holy Spirit with shouting and "joy unspeakable and full of Glory".

I have never forgotten those words that I heard in the Spirit that night; "I want to meet them with the same intensity they have come to meet me." God is still looking for people whose hearts are passionately turned towards Him seeking

His face. He wants to meet you with the same passion and desire that you are directing towards Him.

*"Father, we are your Temple. Father, I am your Temple. Fill Your Temple with Your Glory, now!"*

# Postscript

The personal and theological implications of the Glory of the Lord run much deeper than the scope of this book, however, I hope it has started you on a journey from "glory to glory". There are some observations I would like to make in closing that will help launch you into further realms of glory.

I believe that we have totally underestimated the importance and commonality of Glory Encounters as they relate to the experience of normal New Testament Christianity. Whatever name you choose to give it, the early Christians were first led into a supernatural personal revelatory experience with the Holy Spirit through the name of Jesus Christ. That experience became the foundation for every thing else that happened in their lives from that point forward.

*"Grace and peace be multiplied to you in the knowledge of God and of Jesus Christ our Lord, as His divine power has given to us all things that pertain to life and godliness, through the knowledge of Him who <u>called us by glory</u> and virtue, by which have been given to us exceedingly great and precious promises, that through these you may be partakers of the divine nature, having escaped the corruption that is in the world through lust." 2 Peter 1:2-4 (NKJV)*

The epistles of the New Testament were written by the Apostles back to people that already had the bond of a common experience. They were written for the purpose of growth and edification in that experience. In contrast, much of the efforts of modern Christianity is to use the epistles as requirements on how to achieve the results that were present from the very beginning of the walk during the early days of the Church. We are trying to educate people into an experience while in the Early Church, the Apostles and Evangelist released the power and led the people into the experience first. The early believers had the advantage of the inner working of personal revelation from the Father from the start of their walk rather than trying to derive understanding through human logic and reason as is most often the case today.

The reason many modern Christians fail to experience the Glory of the Lord is that they are trying desperately to earn the right to this encounter through diligent study, human knowledge or formulas and procedures followed in the flesh. In the Acts Church the darkest sinners had a supernatural encounter with the Glory of the Lord first. The transformation produced an immediate effect. The early uneducated and unqualified believers began to immediately operate in the gifts of the Holy Spirit. They had more understanding and power than most modern believers possess after a lifetime of study and preparation for a graduation and commencement type event that never occurs.

It was a common experience of the Holy Spirit that gave them unity.

- ***Ephesians 4:3 "Endeavoring to keep the unity of the Spirit in the bond of peace."***

It was the common experience that gave them revelation.

- ***Mat 16:17** "And Jesus answered and said unto him, Blessed art thou, Simon Bar-jona: for flesh and blood hath not revealed it unto thee, but my Father which is in heaven."*

It was the common experience that gave them power.

- ***Acts 1:8** " But ye shall receive power, after that the Holy Ghost is come upon you: and ye shall be witnesses unto me both in Jerusalem, and in all Judea, and in Samaria, and unto the uttermost part of the earth."*

It was the common experience that became the theological standard by which all new experiences and issues were settled.

- ***Acts 11:15-18** " And as I began to speak, the Holy Ghost fell on them, as on us at the beginning.*
  *Then remembered I the word of the Lord, how that he said, John indeed baptized with water; but ye shall be baptized with the Holy Ghost.*
  *Forasmuch then as God gave them the like gift as he did unto us, who believed on the Lord Jesus Christ; what was I, that I could withstand God?*
  *When they heard these things, they held their peace, and glorified God, saying, Then hath God also to the Gentiles granted repentance unto life."*

If our goal now is to recapture the life, love, power and purity of the New Testament Church, then I believe we must personally and corporately begin to flow in the "glory to glory" experiential and revelatory realm that was the foundation of the Early Church. That's what I call *revival!*

## About the Author

*Author Larry Taylor has spent the past twelve years discovering the present day reality of God's transforming glory. First as a personal touch and then in revival meetings large and small, the glory of God is the driving force of the ministry of the Holy Spirit through Larry.*

*Larry is an ordained Southern Baptist minister who has been used of God as an evangelist, pastor and revivalist since 1971. The world wide scope of his vision and ministry have given him the opportunity to see the transformational power of real glory encounters in cultures on three continents and in settings from small home groups to city wide revivals.*

*Speaking from a strong biblical background as well as amazing personal encounters, Larry makes the subject of God's glory accessible to every reader.*

*Larry is a native Texan whose home is in Fort Worth. He and his wife of 32 years, Carol, travel though out the world ministering the message of the Glory of God revealed in the face of Jesus Christ.*

*Visit the author's website: www.goinministries.org.*

Printed in the United States
57024LVS00001B/13-15